The Death of Amy Robsart

An Elizabethan Mystery

The Death of Amy Robsart

An Elizabethan Mystery

Sarah-Beth Watkins

Winchester, UK
Washington, USA

JOHN HUNT PUBLISHING

First published by Chronos Books, 2020
Chronos Books is an imprint of John Hunt Publishing Ltd., No. 3 East St., Alresford, Hampshire SO24 9EE, UK
office@jhpbooks.com
www.johnhuntpublishing.com
www.chronosbooks.com

For distributor details and how to order please visit the 'Ordering' section on our website.

ISBN: 978 1 78904 482 9
978 1 78904 483 6 (ebook)
Library of Congress Control Number: 2019951191

A CIP catalogue record for this book is available from the British Library.

Design: Stuart Davies

UK: Printed and bound by CPI Group (UK) Ltd, Croydon, CR0 4YY
US: Printed and bound by Thomson-Shore, 7300 West Joy Road, Dexter, MI 48130

Contents

Also by Sarah-Beth Watkins

Lady Katherine Knollys: The Unacknowledged Daughter of King Henry VIII

The Tudor Brandons: Mary and Charles – Henry VIII's Nearest & Dearest

Margaret Tudor, Queen of Scots: The Life of King Henry VIII's Sister

Anne of Cleves: Henry VIII's Unwanted Wife

Catherine of Braganza: Charles II's Restoration Queen

The Tragic Daughters of Charles I

Sir Francis Bryan: Henry VIII's Most Notorious Ambassador
Ireland's Suffragettes

Books for Writers:

Telling Life's Tales

Life Coaching for Writers

The Lifestyle Writer

The Writer's Internet

O worthless sacrifice to pow'r and pride!
O sacred name of honour vilified'
For this—to peril, woe and wrong, betray'd,
No voice to comfort, and no arm to aid,
Herself a stranger in her own wide halls,
Herself a captive in her castle-walls,
And e'en from these by brutal menace torn,
The bride of Leicester lives alone to mourn.

From *Amy Robsart, Emma and Other Poems* by Nicholas Lee Torré

Chapter One

The Wife of Elizabeth I's Favourite

Amy Robsart, wife of Elizabeth I's favourite, Robert Dudley, later the Earl of Leicester, was found dead at the bottom of a flight of stairs on 8 September 1560 at Cumnor Place, near Oxford. Her neck was broken.

Amy was twenty-eight when she died and her marriage to Dudley had been one of great absences and loneliness. Queen Elizabeth I had commanded much of his attention over the past years and Amy had lived a peripatetic life, moving from one house to another, without ever having a home of her own.

What may have been a simple accident has confounded historians for years with its inconsistencies. There are more questions than answers. Was it an accident, suicide or murder? We'll take a look at Amy's background, the circumstances surrounding her death and weigh up the evidence for each case.

* * *

Amy was the daughter of Sir John Robsart and Elizabeth Scott of Stanfield Hall near Wymondham in Norfolk. It was here that she first met the dashingly handsome Robert Dudley with his father and his brothers John and Ambrose on their way to subdue Kett's Rebellion – a revolt that stemmed from the enclosure of common fields by wealthy landowners. Sir John Robsart had allowed the army to camp in his grounds and provided an evening meal for the senior officers. Amy was in attendance and it was then that she met the man she would soon marry.

Robert wed Amy the next year when she was only seventeen on 4 June 1550 at Sheen. Instead of it being just an arranged match, there were definitely feelings of love (or lust) as William

Cecil, Elizabeth I's chief advisor, called Dudley and Amy's 'a carnal marriage'.[1] Amy was of a lower social status than Robert but she was his choice and one accepted by his family. Their wedding ceremony came after the more auspicious marriage of his elder brother John to Anne Seymour, the eldest daughter of Edward Seymour, 1st Duke of Somerset and former Lord Protector of England. Nevertheless the weekend was a round of entertainment presided over by the young king, Edward VI.

Robert Dudley came from a family that had the taint of scandal attached to it. His grandfather, Edmund Dudley, had been Henry VII's financial advisor and was one of the first people that Henry VIII executed when he came to power. His father too would succumb to the wrath of a sovereign.

When Edward VI knew he was dying, he wrote his 'Devise for the Succession' that disinherited his sisters, Mary and Elizabeth. He had hoped to pass the throne on to the male descendants of Frances Brandon, the Duchess of Suffolk, and failing that, to the male heirs of the Lady Jane Grey, but neither of them had any male children by the time of Edward's demise. Edward rejected the idea that a woman could reign by herself but on his deathbed his cousin Lady Jane was named his heir. Jane never wanted such majesty thrust upon her. But John Dudley, Robert's father and Jane's father-in-law, moved to place her on the throne and sent his sons to place the Princess Mary in custody.

Mary was wise to their machinations and escaped their clutches, rallying her supporters and proclaiming her right to the throne. She was crowned the rightful Queen of England on 1 October 1553 at Westminster Abbey and Jane was taken to the Tower of London along with those who had worked to make her queen.

Dudley senior was attainted as a traitor and executed in 1553 on Tower Hill. His five sons were imprisoned awaiting trial. Guildford, as Jane's husband would be executed along with his wife but John, Ambrose, Robert and Henry would remain in the

Tower for a time.

Amy saw her husband through his imprisonment in the Tower, visiting him as the other wives visited his brothers. The Lieutenant of the Tower had received an order 'to permit these ladies to have access unto their husbands, and there to tarry with them so long and at such times as by him shall be thought meet'. John would be released due to ill health but died three days later. Ambrose, Robert and Henry were released in 1554.

Amy and Robert had had very little money in the early days of their marriage until on the death of Queen Mary, Elizabeth I gained her crown and Dudley was made Master of Horse, a position once held by his older brother, Ambrose. Dudley and Elizabeth had known each other for many years perhaps from when Elizabeth was as young as eight years old and at the court of her father Henry VIII. She had also spent time in the Tower as he had done and their bond would become unbreakable.

Dudley was by her side when she first officially entered the city of London on 28 November 1558 and he was there again for her coronation. He would be by her side whenever she wanted him and that would turn out to be quite a lot.

In the early days of Elizabeth's reign there was much speculation about who the queen would marry. The Spanish ambassador was there to push King Philip's suit, her sister Mary's husband, but by December he was writing 'Everybody thinks that she will not marry a foreigner, and they cannot make out whom she favours, so that every day some new cry is raised about a husband'.[2] But by April he knew who was most favoured by the queen when he reported 'Lord Robert has come so much into favour that he does whatever he likes with affairs. It is even said that Her Majesty visits him in his chamber day and night'.[3]

Elizabeth was enjoying her freedom and her liberty. She was surrounded by female attendants but also Robert who in his role as Master of Horse made sure she had the best horses to ride out on every day and accompanied her wherever she went.

There was a proposal from Eric of Sweden, the aging Earl of Arundel was keen and Elizabeth had even hinted she would marry into Scotland to 'give the King of France some trouble'.[4] But while she countered ambassador's proposals and deflected the pleas of her council, she moved Dudley into apartments next to her own and spent her days in his company. And it did not go unnoticed. The Spanish ambassador wrote 'it is generally stated that it is his (Dudley's) fault that the Queen does not marry' and he also noted that she was playing with fire 'if she marry the said Mylord Robert, she will incur so much enmity that she may one evening lay herself down as Queen of England and rise up the next morning as plain Madam Elizabeth ... it is a marvel that he has not been slain long ere this'.[5]

Kat Ashley, Elizabeth's chief lady of the bedchamber, had been with the queen since childhood and she was worried about her unbreakable affection for Robert Dudley. Kat had seen how flirtations could turn sour as when Elizabeth and Thomas Seymour had become too close.

Elizabeth had lived for a time with Henry VIII's last wife, Katherine Parr, the Dowager Queen, and her last husband the Lord High Admiral, Sir Thomas Seymour. Seymour would steal the key to the princess's bedchamber and startle her in the early hours of the morning when he would pretend to jump on her whilst she was still in bed. If she was up but not dressed, he became too familiar with her and would slap her bottom whilst wearing nothing but his nightshirt. Seymour stole kisses from Elizabeth and flirted with her shamelessly whilst his wife, Katherine, looked on and even held Elizabeth down when her husband cut the princess's dress to shreds one day whilst they were walking in the gardens.

Elizabeth was eventually sent to live with Sir Anthony Denny but Seymour began to talk of marrying her after his wife's death and was subsequently arrested. Kat Ashley followed him to the Tower to be questioned over Elizabeth's conduct. It was an experience she would never forget and now that her mistress was queen, Kat feared what would happen if Elizabeth continued to place Dudley before all others.

Kat was an astute woman and she heard the rumours spreading, saw the looks aimed at Dudley and feared civil war was brewing. She told Elizabeth that her behaviour towards her favourite 'occasioned much evil speaking' and begged her to marry someone else to protect her 'honour and dignity'.[6]

Elizabeth knew Kat spoke from the heart but she was not impressed with her outburst nor the suggestion she give up her favourite. She said that she had given

> *no one just cause to associate her with her Equerry or any other man in the world, and she hoped that they never would truthfully be able to do so. But that in this world she had so much sorrow and tribulation and so little joy. If she showed herself gracious towards her Master of the Horse she had deserved it for his honourable nature and dealings ... She was always surrounded by her ladies of the bedchamber and maids of honour, who at all times could see whether there was anything dishonourable between her and her Master of the Horse. If she had ever had the will or had found pleasure in such a dishonourable life ... she did not know of anyone who could forbid her...*[7]

Elizabeth made no apologies for her relationship with Dudley and was not about to change her ways. The new Spanish ambassador, Bishop Alvaro de la Quadra, echoed his predecessor's warnings about her favourite writing 'there is not a man in England who does not cry out upon him as the Queen's ruin'.[8]

Elizabeth steadfastly refused to take a husband even though her council constantly pressured her to. In order to secure the succession, they felt she should marry and have children but it was a path Elizabeth refused to take. There are many theories why – from the loss of her mother Anne Boleyn by execution to her brief flirtation with Thomas Seymour and subsequent removal from his household and her overwhelming fear of childbirth.

But even though she was the virgin queen, she was not immune to the attentions of a good-looking man. Amy's husband, Robert Dudley, who she nicknamed Sweet Robin and 'her eyes', was everything to her. There was much speculation as to how close they really were and it was whispered that they were lovers but Elizabeth, although showering her favourite with affection, refused to be drawn into admitting any relationship saying 'a thousand eyes see all I do'.[9]

Dudley didn't often have time for his wife. The court and the queen commanded his attendance almost constantly but that did not mean that he forgot about Amy. He tried to visit and sent gifts of clothes, money and jewels. Elizabeth was wildly jealous of any of her favourite's relationships and commanded Dudley to say he did nothing with his wife. It was not overtly stated but Amy was not welcome at court and when she travelled to London to see Robert she stayed in other accommodation.

There had been an attempt to buy Dudley Castle, Robert's family home and somewhere where Amy could have run her own household but it fell through. Instead she stayed mostly at William Hyde's house in Throcking at least between 1557 and 1559. In the year before her death, Amy was staying there and Dudley visited her at Easter. He brought with him cooks, food and expensive spices so they would eat well.

Amy then travelled to London, to Camberwell and her mother's family home. Dudley was not there to meet her as he had left for Windsor and his investiture as a knight of the garter but on his return they spent time together. She also took a trip to Suffolk sometime this year and it is possible that she then moved to Sir Richard Verney's home, Compton Verney in Warwickshire, before finally settling at Cumnor Place in December 1559.

Amy's movements are important because they show a young

woman in good health, able to travel around the country visiting family and friends until she took up residence at her final home.

Cumnor Place was built in the fourteenth century of grey stone and had been used as a monastic summer retreat. It had once belonged to Dr George Owen, a royal physician who had passed it on to William Owen, his son who now rented it to Anthony Forster, Dudley's steward of personal expenses. Forster lived there with his family and it was also home to Ann Owen, the widow of Dr George Owen and Elizabeth Odingsells, the widowed sister of William Hyde of Denchworth.

Amy would move in with her maid Mrs Picto, William Huggins and other retainers whilst her husband would be three miles away at Windsor Castle. Cumnor Place was a substantial manor house of four wings around an inner courtyard. It was set in copious grounds with a garden, fish pond and deer park. It had a long gallery and a great hall where its occupants met for meals and entertainment. Her chamber was the best in the house, south-east of the great hall with its own entrance and stairway – a room fit for a lady albeit one that rarely saw her husband and longed for her own home.

On that fatal day in September Amy was adamant that everyone should attend Abingdon Fair, 'she would not that day suffer one of her own sort to tarry at home, and was so earnest to have them gone'.[10] She however would remain in the house. The fair was a yearly occasion to celebrate the feast of Our Lady spread over the weekend but Mrs Odingsells didn't want to go on a day when all the servants attended 'she said it was no day for gentlewomen to go in, but said the morrow was much better, and then she would go'. Amy was not happy and became 'very angry'[11] with her. When asked who would keep her company, Amy said she would dine with old Mrs Owen.

Amy was left to her own devices and was insistent she wanted to be left alone. By the time the household returned home that evening Amy was dead.

Chapter Two

The Ambassador's Reports

Amy was dead and there would have to be an investigation into how and why but the rumour mill had been turning for some time about Dudley and his wife.

The Spanish ambassador, Count de Feria had written in April 1559:

Lord Robert has come to so much into favour that he does whatever he likes with affairs and It is even said that her majesty visits him in his chamber day and night. People talk of this so freely that they go so far as to say that his wife has a malady in one of her breasts and the Queen is only waiting for her to die to marry Lord Robert.[1]

The Venetian ambassador also believed Amy 'had been ailing for some time' when he wrote in May. And added that if she 'were perchance to die, the Queen might easily take him (Dudley) for her husband'.[2]

But the Spanish ambassador Bishop de la Quadra reported that Amy was 'already much better'. However come November he was also saying that 'Lord Robert has sent to poison his wife'. He felt that the queen was stalling over a potential marriage 'until this wicked deed of killing his wife is consummated'.[3]

Caspar von Breuner, the Imperial ambassador also reported 'It is said that he seeks to poison his wife, for he is indeed a great favourite with the Queen' and

Although he is married to a beautiful wife he is not living with her, and, as I have been told by many persons, is trying to do away with her by poison. For this reason I think that the Queen and he have a secret understanding, for I know full well … that the Queen had

> *more than once been addressed and entreated by various persons to exercise more prudence and not give people cause to suspect her in connection with this man, whereat she with many oaths exculpated herself. I now hear that the liking grows in intensity with the lapse of time.*[4]

Bruener was no friend to Dudley and saw that many at court would not accept him should the queen decide to make him her husband.

> *I really do believe that he will follow in the footsteps of his parents, and may the Devil be his companion, for he causes me and all those who are active on behalf of his Princely Highness a world of trouble. He is so hated by the Knights and Commoners that it is a marvel that he has not been slain long ere this, for whenever they behold him they wish he might be hanged. An Englishman once asked if England was so poor that none could be found to stab him with a poniard. But I am certain that he will one day meet with the reward he so richly merits. It is just like him to protract this marriage until he has sent his wife into Eternity.*[5]

By March 1560 Quadra was echoing Bruner's thoughts.

> *He is the worst and most procrastinating young man I ever saw in my life, and not at all courageous or spirited. I have brought all the artillery I can to bear upon him, and, by my faith if it were not for some fear of our own house I would soon give the historians something to talk about. Not a man in England but cries at the top of his voice that this fellow is ruining the country with his vanity.*[6]

He then reported he had heard that Dudley 'told somebody, who has not kept silence, that if he live another year he will be in a very different position from now. He is laying in a good stock or arms, and is assuming every day a more masterful part in affairs.

They say he thinks of divorcing his wife'.[7]

And so the rumours continued…

Chapter Three

The Aftermath

Robert Dudley was told the news of his wife's death by Bowes, a servant, who had been present when Amy's body was found. Dudley wrote to his man Blount:

> *Cousin Blount, immediately upon your departing from me there came to me Bowes, by whom I do understand that my wife is dead, and, as he saith, by a fall from a pair of stairs. Little other understanding can I have of him. The greatness and the suddenness of the misfortune doth so perplex me, until I do hear from you how the matter standeth, or how this evil should light upon me, considering what the malicious world will bruit, as I can take no rest. And because I have no way to purge myself of the malicious talk that I know the wicked world will use, but one which is the very plain truth to be known, I do pray you, as you have loved me, and do tender me and my quietness, and as now my special trust is in you, that (you) will use all the devises and means you can possible for the learning of the truth; wherein have no respect for any living person. And as by your own travail and diligence, so likewise by order of law, I mean by calling of the Coroner, and charging him to the uttermost from me to have good regard to make choice of no light or slight persons, but the discreetest and substantial men, for the juries, such as for their knowledge may be able to search thoroughly and duly, by all manner of examinations, the bottom of the matter, and for their uprightness will earnestly and sincerely deal therein without respect; and that the body be viewed and searched accordingly by them; and in every respect to proceed by order and law. In the mean time, Cousin Blount, let me be advertised from you by this bearer with all speed how the matter doth stand. For, as the cause and the manner thereof doth*

> *marvellously trouble me, considering my case, many ways, so shall I not be at rest till I may be ascertained thereof; praying you, even as my trust is in you, and as I have ever loved you, do not dissemble with me, neither let anything be hid from me, but send me your true conceit and opinion of the matter, whether it happened by evil chance or by villainy. And fail not to let me hear continually from you*[1]

Dudley signed the letter as 'much perplexed' and also told Blount that he had sent for Amy's half-brother, John Appleyard and other of her friends to 'see how all things do proceed'.

Blount was on the way to Cumnor when he received the letter. He immediately wrote back he had received it and assured Dudley he would endeavour to find a 'true understanding of the matter'.[2] But instead of riding straight to Cumnor he decided to stop at an inn in Abingdon and find out what the rumours were. There he asked the innkeeper for any news.

> *He said, there was fallen a great misfortune within three or four miles of the town; he said my Lord Robert Dudley's wife was dead, and I asked him what was his judgement, and the judgement of the people; he said some were disposed to say well and some evil.*[3]

Blount asked him what he thought of the situation.

> *I judge it a misfortune, because it chanced in that honest gentleman's house, his great honesty … doth much curb the evil thoughts of the people.*[4]

The innkeeper was referring to Anthony Forster who was popular with the local people and known to be an honest and fair man.

Dudley had asked Blount to ensure an inquest was held with a jury of the 'discreetest and substantial men' to 'search thoroughly and duly, by all matter of examinations, the bottom of the matter'.[5] By the time Blount got to Cumnor the inquest was already under way and the jury already chosen with the local coroner presiding. Blount assured Dudley:

But to the inquest you would have so very circumspectly chosen by the coroner for the understanding of the truth, your Lordship needeth not doubt of their well choosing ... If I be able to judge of men and of their ableness, I judge them and specially some of them, to be as wise and as able men to be chosen upon such a matter as any men...[6]

Not all of the men were fans of Anthony Forster but Blount felt that that was all the better for if there was a hint of foul play they would uncover it.

Dudley was anxious to know what had befallen his wife telling Blount he could not be 'in quiet' until he heard. He definitely thought that Amy might have been the victim of a crime. He wanted the jury to say if it were chance or misfortune and if it appeared to be 'villiany (as God forbid so mischievous or wicked a body should live) then to find it so'.[7] He was also thinking of himself when he wrote

God willing I shall never fear the dire prosecution accordingly, what person soever it may appear any way to touch; as well for the just punishment of the act as for mine own true justification, for as I would (be) sorry in my heart any such evil should be committed, so shall it well appear to the world my innocency by my dealing in the matter, if it shall so fall out.[8]

Blount wrote back to tell Dudley, who at the queen's insistence, had moved to his house at Kew, a gift from Elizabeth, that the jury

be very secret, and yet do I hear a whispering that they can find

> *no presumptions of evil. And if I may say to your Lordship my conscience: I think some of them be sorry for it, God forgive me. … Mine own opinion is much quieted, the more I search of it, the more free it doth appear to me … the circumstances and as many things as I can learn doth persuade me that only misfortune hath done it, and nothing else.*[9]

The jury would come to rule that it had all been a dreadful accident.

But for now Dudley felt like he was on shaky ground. His exile in Kew took him away from his queen and he feared what this would mean for their relationship. William Cecil visited him there one evening and from the letter that Dudley rushed off to him the next day, full of mistakes, it appears he was in shock:

> *Sir, I thank you very much for your being hear, and the great frendshipp you have shewyd towards me I shall not forget. I am veary loath to wysh you hear againe, but I wold be very glad to be with you thear. I pray you let me hear from you, what you think best for me to doe. If you dowbt, I pray you ask the question, for the soner you can advyse me thether, the more I shall thank you. I am sorry so sodden a chaunce shald breede me so great a chandge, for methinks I am hear all this while as it wear in a dreame, and to farr, to farre from the place I am bound to be, where, mythinkes also, this long, idle tyme can not excuse me for the dewty I have to discharge ells whear. I pray you help him that seues to be at liberty owt of so great bondage. Forget me not, though you se me not, and I will remember you and fayll ye not, and so wysh you well to doe… I besech your Sir, forget not to offer up he humble sacrafyce you promysed me.*[10]

Meanwhile those ambassadors who had speculated on Amy's death now had something more to report. Quadra's next letter written on 11 September contained some startling revelations.

When talking to William Cecil, Elizabeth I's chief advisor, he said that the Queen and Dudley 'were thinking of destroying Lord Robert's wife. They had given out that she was ill; but she was not ill at all, she was very well, and taking care not to be poisoned'.[11] So he was repeating what he had previously said about poison and illness but this time he had mentioned Cecil and the queen. He also said that the queen 'on her return from hunting, told me that the Lord Robert's wife was dead, or nearly so, and begged me to say nothing about it'.[12] Elizabeth apparently told Quadra this before making a public declaration but we can assume that as soon as Dudley knew of Amy's death she was informed and had told the ambassador prior to making a formal statement. That she said Amy was 'nearly so' points to her not knowing any details.

Elizabeth I ordered the court into mourning and it was noted that Dudley and his friends and family were all dressed in black and weeping but that 'great hypocrisy was used'.[13]

Was William Cecil being a hypocrite too? He had purposely given the Spanish ambassador reason to suspect Dudley of being involved in his wife's death. Or had he? Was Quadra lying or was Cecil really trying to make sure that the scandal was so great that Dudley could never marry the queen. Cecil had strived for so long to get Elizabeth to marry for the good of the country and the succession of the monarchy.

The queen's chief advisor was definitely frustrated. He had left Elizabeth to travel north that summer to build an alliance with the Scots. His negotiations had gone well but on his return Elizabeth was dismissive and he could plainly see how much more intimate she and Dudley had become. He was afraid that if Dudley got his way and became king consort, Elizabeth would no longer need her loyal advisor. But now, with Amy's death, both the queen and Dudley needed him more than ever.

Amy's body was duly removed to Gloucester College where she lay in state for mourners to pay their respects. The rooms there were draped in black and she lay under both Dudley's and her family's arms. The procession to the church of St Mary's, Oxford for her burial on 22 September was led by two conductors bearing black staves followed by eighty poor men and women dressed in black. Amy's half-brother John Appleyard walked in front of her coffin, carried by eight yeomen, and attended by two royal heralds whom Dudley had paid over £66 to oversee and record the funeral.

Lady Margery Norris, the queen's companion, was chief mourner followed by six women from Cumnor; Mrs Wayneman, Lady Pollard, Mrs Doylly, Mrs Butler, Mrs Blunt and Elizabeth Mutlowe, and many others who followed behind.

Dudley made sure no expense was spared and paid for a funeral costing around £2000. The church had been draped in black cloth and a hearse or wooden frame had been constructed in which to place her coffin, decorated with escutcheons of arms and a black valance 'written with letters of gold and fringed with a fringe of black silk'.[14] Dr Francis Babington, doctor of divinity and master of Balliol College gave the sermon. It was later said that he 'tript once or twice by recommending to his auditors the virtues of that lady so pitifully murdered instead of so pitifully slain'.[15] Dudley did not attend as was customary nor did he arrange for a memorial to be built for her but he stayed in mourning for six months.

Chapter Four

Rumours Surround the Queen

Within days the news of Amy's death reached the courts abroad.

Sir Nicholas Throckmorton, the English ambassador in France, and a friend of Dudley's, wrote to him to offer his condolences but he also wrote to the Marquis of Northampton to tell him of the 'dishonorable and naughty reports that are here made of ye Queen's Majesty'.[1] The French court was alive with suspicion and rumour. Throckmorton continued:

> *I am almost at my wits end and know not what to say: one laugheth at us, another threateneth, another revileth her Majesty and some let not say what religion is this that a subject shall kill his wife, and ye Prince not only bear withal but marry with him … Alas that I ever lived to see this day. All the estimation we had got clean is gone and the infamy passeth the same so far, as my heart bleedeth to think upon the slanderous bruits I hear, which if they be not slaked or that they prove true, our reputation is gone forever, war followeth and utter subversion of our green country. Help my Lord to slake these rumours, and let honour remain where it ought to be …*[2]

Throckmorton was panicking and he sent off more letters to Cecil, the Earls of Pembroke and Bedford, Northampton and the Lord Admiral. The situation in France was dire and he also wrote to his friend Henry Killigrew who tried to calm him with his reply:

> *I cannot imagine what rumours they be you hear there, as you write so strange. Unless such were here of the death of my Lady Dudley; for that she brake her neck down a pair of stairs, which I protest*

> *unto you was only done by the hand of God, to my knowledge.*[3]

But Throckmorton was still worried, frantically so, convinced that if the queen were to marry Dudley the country would be ruined and on the brink of civil war. He sent his man Robert Jones over to see the queen in person to impress upon her the risk she ran by entertaining any notions of marrying Dudley now his wife was gone. Jones arrived at court on 25 November and the following day Dudley sent him a message he wanted to meet with him in secret. He had heard Jones's reports and was raging at the news that Mary, Queen of Scots had remarked that the queen would marry 'her horse-keeper'. Dudley wanted to know if those were Jones's words but the man told him 'that the French queen had said that the Queen would marry the Master of her horses'.[4] Slightly different wording but it meant much to Elizabeth's favourite.

On 27 November 1560, Elizabeth granted Jones a private audience and when he brought up Throckmorton's fears of her marrying Dudley she wearily told him she had heard it all before. Jones reported to the ambassador:

> *She thereupon told me, that the matter had been tried in the country, and found to be contrary to that which was reported, saying that he (Dudley) was then in the Court, and none of his at the attempt at his wife's house; and that it fell out as should neither touch his honesty nor her honour.*[5]

Both of the phrases *that he was then in the Court, and none of his at the attempt at his wife's house* and *touch his honesty nor her honour* were written in cipher.

What did the queen mean by 'attempt'? Did she know something more sinister about Amy's death?

She seemed so sure that Dudley had no part in whatever had happened and that the rumours and suspicion would die down but Throckmorton was not done. He continued to write letters to those around her including Cecil. It was imperative that the queen did nothing to add fuel to the fire and any notions of a Dudley marriage must stop.

It seems that the queen started to listen. She had been planning to raise her Master of Horse to the peerage as once her father had done with Anne Boleyn but she realised that now was not the time. Jones let Throckmorton know:

> *The Queen's Majesty stayeth the creation. The bills were made for the purpose, at the day appointed. When they were presented, she with a knife cut them asunder. I can by no means learn, and yet I have talked with such as know much, that my Lord Robert's matters will not go, as was looked for; and yet the favours be great which are showed him at the Queen's Majesty's hands.*[6]

Elizabeth would never marry Dudley but she was not happy at having her hand and mind forced. Cecil saw that her anger might soon turn on those that had advised her and he wrote to Throckmorton:

> *I must advise you not to meddle with the matters of this court otherwise than ye may be well advised from hence. What her Majesty will determine to do only God I think knoweth ... But in one word I say contend not where victory cannot be had.*[7]

Others urged him to leave well alone and Throckmorton took their advice. He would never write about the circumstances surrounding Amy's death and of her husband again.

Chapter Five

The Coroner's Report

The verdict on Amy's death was not given until the local Berkshire Assizes in August 1561 and it wouldn't be until over four hundred years later, in 2008, that the coroner's report was found in the National Archives at Kew. It reads thus:

> *The aforesaid Lady Amy on 8 September in the aforesaid second year of the reign of the said lady queen (Elizabeth), being alone in a certain chamber within the home of a ceratin Anthony Forster, Esq., in the aforesaid Cumnor, and intending to descend the aforesaid chamber by way of certain steps (in English called 'steyres') of the aforesaid chamber there and then accidentally fell precipitously down the aforesaid steps to the very bottom of the same steps, through which the same Lady Amy there and then sustained not only two injuries to her head (in English called 'dyntes') – one of which was a quarter of an inch deep and the other two inches deep – but truly also, by reason of the accidental injury or of that fall and of Lady Amy's own body weight falling down, the aforesaid stairs, the same Lady Amy there and then broke her own neck, on account of which certain fracture of the neck the same Lady Amy there and then died instantly; and the aforesaid Lady Amy was found there and then without any other mark or wound on her body; and thus the jurors say on their oath that the aforesaid Lady Amy in the manner and form aforesaid by misfortune came to her death and not otherwise, in so far as it is possible at present for them to agree; in testimony of which fact for this inquest both the aforesaid coroner and also the aforesaid jurors have in turn affixed their seals on the day.*[1]

So Amy also had head wounds – two in fact, one of which was

severe. A Spanish report had mentioned she was found with a dagger in her head but this was blatantly untrue. Was her death then truly an accident or could there have been more to it? The sentence 'by misfortune came to her death and not otherwise, in so far as it is possible at present for them to agree…' is also ambiguous. Did some of the jury have their doubts?

Chapter Six

Accident?

We might think that a slight fall down some stairs would leave you with nothing more than a few bruises. Amy had none of those. No marks on her body at all apart from her head wounds.

Then you would think it would depend on how far you fell.

Amy fell down eight steps on a pair of stairs so two flights broken by a landing but we don't know if she was found on the landing or at the foot of the stairs nor what position her body was in. A description of Cumnor Place describes the stairs as a 'circular newel stone staircase'[1] where from the midpoint landing the stairs continued by 180 degrees.

The stairs were stone and she quite possibly smacked her head on their worn edges on her way down leaving the two 'deyntes' in her head or her head struck a wall sconce or other protrusion. There was no mention of blood which two head wounds would have created.

Leicester's Commonwealth printed much later would tell the story that Amy's headdress was found 'without hurting of her hood that stood upon her head'[2] but that seems to be pure fiction. There is no mention in the coroner's report of how she was found, the position of her body or what she was wearing.

In fact deaths from falling down stairs are more common than you would like to think. It is estimated that someone falls down the stairs in the UK every ninety seconds and while most accidents are not fatal, in 2015 787 deaths in England and Wales were caused by such a fall.[3] Hitting your head is also one of the most common injuries sustained from such an accident.

It had been reported that Amy had a malady of the breast but also that she was better. If she had had breast cancer it may have contributed to her neck breaking so easily.

In 1956 an eminent professor Ian Aird writing in the *English Historical Review* suggested that Amy's death could have been due to a weakening of her bones caused by breast cancer. He had read that Amy had died with her hood still upon her head which prompted him to investigate how that could come to be. Aird suggested that cancer deposits on the spine cause brittle bones that can break under stress and a simple act such as walking down stairs or a short fall can make them snap.

Spontaneous fracture of the spine, or of any bone, occurs when the bone, weakened and softened by disease or age, collapses or breaks under the strain of normal muscular effort ... Diseased or aged bones in the spine may collapse from the slight strain imposed upon them by the normal act of stepping, for example. If that part of the spine which lies in the neck (cervical spine) suffers in this way, the affected person gets spontaneously 'a broken neck', and may collapse then, totally paralysed from the neck down or suddenly dead. Such a fracture is more likely to occur in stepping downstairs than in walking on the level.[4]

But surely if Amy was so weak there would have been other symptoms and Dudley would have known she was ill. The Spanish ambassador Bishop de la Quadra reported that she was better. So if she had had breast cancer – and we don't know that for sure – she was recovering. Her movements prior to moving to Cumnor Place, her travels and visits to friends and family, were not that of a sick woman. When she was found dead, Dudley was shocked and insistent on an investigation. If he had known she was ill, would he have been so frantic to find out how she died?

Only one letter extant written by Henry Hastings, the Earl of Huntingdon to Dudley hints at Amy's 'trouble'.

As I ended my letter I understood by letters the death of my lady your wife. I doubt not but long before this time you have considered what a happy hour it is which bringeth man from sorrow to joy, from mortality to immortality, from care and trouble to rest and quietness, and that the Lord above worketh all the best to them that love him.[5]

What 'care and trouble' was Amy now at peace from? Could it be that Hastings knew of her illness or perhaps he was referring to her having a troubled mind. We shall look at that suggestion in the next chapter.

Other medical theories put forward of an aortic aneurism, cervical spondylosis or tuberculosis of the spine cannot be proved.

At the time nobody really seemed to have believed it was an accident apart from the jury who ruled it so. There was no mention of blood which surely with two head wounds, one of which was two thumbs deep, there should have been. Had she been killed elsewhere and her body placed at the foot of the stairs to make it look like an accident?

That wound and its deepness stick out as being odd. We don't know where the wounds were exactly but something so deep that it had penetrated the skull and into the brain speak to something more sinister. Even the term used in the coroner's report 'deyntes' is more typically associated with a blow or wound due to violence.

People were much more inclined to suspect foul play or suggest that perhaps Amy had sought to end her own life.

Chapter Seven

Suicide?

In August Amy wanted a dress made for her and wrote:

> *Edney, with my hearty commendations this shall be to desire you to take the pains for me as to make this gown of velvet which I send you with such a collar as you made my russet taffeta gown you sent me last, & I will see you discharged for all. I pray you let it be done with as much speed as you can & sent by this bearer Frewen the carrier of Oxford, & thus I bid you most heartily farewell from Cumnor this 24th of August.*
> *Your assured friend,*
> *Amy Dudley.*[1]

This pre-planning proves she was looking to the future and was concerned about her appearance. She wanted the dress made quickly and must have had an occasion in mind when she was to wear it but anything could have happened in the days preceding this letter to plunge her into the depths of despair.

Her marriage had changed from one of love and support to loneliness and rumour. She cannot have been immune to the talk of her husband and the queen and it must have made her unhappy. They had not been blessed with children and she was not in charge of her own home. Amy died on the day after the celebrations for Elizabeth I's twenty-seventh birthday. She had not seen her husband for many months and knew he was at court with the queen constantly by her side. Life was difficult.

Much has been made of a phrase Amy wrote in 1557 when she said she was 'not being altogether in quiet'[2] at the departure of her husband but as author Chris Skidmore has pointed out, it was due to Dudley leaving England to fight the French at the siege of St Quentin. Not only had she been left in charge of estate management but she may also have feared that Dudley would be killed in the fighting.

The evidence that Amy may have committed suicide is scant. Blount wrote to Dudley that he judged Amy 'to be a strange woman of mind' and in the same correspondence reiterates 'truly the tales I do hear of her maketh me to think she had a strange mind in her; as I will tell you at my coming'.[3] But what he went on to tell Dudley we do not know.

Blount had questioned Amy's maid and devoted servant, Mrs Picto, who told him that Amy 'was a good virtuous gentlewoman, and daily would pray upon her knees; and divers times she saith that she had heard (Amy) pray to God to deliver her from desperation'. Blount pressed her – did Amy have an 'evil toy' in her mind? Mrs Picto anxiously replied 'No, good Mr Blount ... do not judge so of my words; if you should so gather, I am sorry I said so much'.[4]

What would Amy need to be delivered from? What would cause her desperation? Her marriage to a man who was enamoured with the queen? A man who may have been planning to divorce her? As we have seen she may have been ill, she may have been in pain or was so scared of being poisoned she had become severely depressed.

Amy was afraid that someone was trying to poison her and had left William Hyde's house in Throcking because she had voiced her fears and 'he desired she might no longer tarry in his house'.[5] The ambassadors, von Breuner and Quadra, had reported that Dudley was poisoning his wife but they hardly knew this to be fact and were just reporting rumours. Regardless of whether Dudley or anyone else was attempting to poison her, Amy may have been so troubled that worry and depression caught hold of her and caused her to take her own life.

Sir Nicholas Throckmorton, the English ambassador in France, wrote to Sir Thomas Chamberlain, 'My friends advise me from home that Lord Robert's wife is dead and hath by mischance broken her neck herself'.[6]

He then crossed out 'herself' and inserted 'own' so it read 'hath by mischance broken her own neck'.

If she wanted to commit suicide, throwing herself down the stairs was not a fool proof way to do it. It could have left her with severe injuries instead. It has been suggested that she would chose this way to make it look like an accident. She had sent all her servants to the fair to give herself the opportunity. But that in itself would look suspicious.

There are lots of reasons why Amy might have considered ending her own life and we will never know what went on in her mind but suicide seems unlikely if we look at Amy's religiosity.

Amy found solace in the Protestant religion and in the sixteenth century to take one's own life was a punishable crime. As there would be no living person to blame the crime upon, it could be taken out on the corpse. One case ruled that the deceased should be carried 'to some cross way near the town's end and there ... have a stake driven through her breast and so be buried with the stake to be seen, for a memorial that others going by, seeing the same, might take heed'.[7]

Amy prayed daily. She would have known that suicide was a mortal sin caused by the devil and endangered the soul to eternal damnation. Suicides were not buried in a churchyard nor allowed a Christian burial service. They were buried typically under the cover of darkness with no mourners present in an undisclosed grave often along a public highway or at a crossroads.

Legally, suicide was termed 'felo de se' – felon of himself. All the possessions, goods, money and property of a person who committed self-murder would be forfeit to the crown. That would mean for Amy that her inheritance of the Robsart lands and all she owned would go to the queen.

Although it was considered by some to be Amy's cause of death, looking at the evidence suicide seems highly unlikely.

Chapter Eight

The Curious Case of John Appleyard

Four months after Amy's death the Spanish ambassador, Quadra, informed King Philip of a talk he had with Henry Sidney:

> *As regards the death of the wife, he was certain that it was accidental, and he had never been able to learn otherwise, although he had inquired with great care and knew that public opinion held to the contrary. I told him if what he said were true the evil was less, for, if murder had been committed, God would never help nor fail to punish so abominable a crime, whatever men might do to mend it but that it would be difficult for Lord Robert to make things appear as he represented them. He answered it was quite true that no one believed it, and that even preachers in the pulpits discoursed on the matter in a way that was prejudicial to the honour and interests of the Queen.*[1]

Henry Sidney may have been convinced of Dudley's innocence but not so Henry Fitzalan, the Earl of Arundel and it was reported in September 1561 that he wanted the case reopened.

Although Arundel was old enough to be Elizabeth's father he had held high hopes of marrying her. He was one of the premier nobles in the land and felt that if she should choose to marry within her kingdom, he would be an excellent match. The Venetian ambassador wrote in January 1559 'some persons declare that she will take the Earl of Arundel, he being the chief peer of this realm. Not withstanding his being old in comparison with the queen. This report is founded on the constant and daily favours he receives in public and private from her majesty'.[2] Although another ambassador would later sarcastically put it 'he and he alone entertains the hope'.[3]

Arundel lived at Nonsuch where he entertained the queen on her first summer progress. He had been instrumental in putting Mary I on the throne and thought that Dudley might take his revenge on him for the earl's part in Dudley's father's death as a traitor.

Arundel, a leading Catholic, was acutely against Dudley marrying the queen, afraid of what he would do if he came into so much power. Arundel could not let that happen and it may have been this that sparked his call for the reinvestigation of Amy's death. His retainer Guntor certainly echoed his master's feelings when he heard from a friend that after Elizabeth had dined with Dudley, she 'fell in talk with them that carried the torches, and said, that her Grace would make their Lord the best that ever was of his name'. Guntor was furious and swore:

> *I think him to be the cause that my Lord my master (Arundel) might not marry the Queen's highness. Wherefore I would that he had been put to death with his father, or that some ruffian would have dispatched him by the way as he hath gone, with some dagger or gun.*[4]

Dudley had words with Arundel but it did nothing to stop the earl from looking further into Amy's death. The Spanish ambassador reported 'the earl went home and he and others are drawing up copies of the testimony given in the inquiry respecting the death of Lord Robert's wife'[5] but it seems as if they could find no new evidence as nothing ever came of his suspicions.

And someone else who was not convinced that Amy's death was an accident was her half-brother from her mother's first marriage, John Appleyard. Arundel as well as Cecil would be amongst the men who would be called upon to examine his allegations.

Back in 1560, Appleyard had been called for as soon as Amy's death was known. Dudley had made sure of that. But he had been since been in contact with Dudley and told him he was 'moved to search'[6] for further answers to his sister's death.

Matters came to a head when Dudley sent his man Blount to him and Appleyard had this story to tell:

> *There came to me a man, as I judge, he said, a waterman, into the garden at Hampton Court, and delivered me a letter wherein I was called to come over the water alone, and there I should find a man alone that had to say to me in great matters, and secret, Whereupon … after debating the matter with himself, [he] went over the water and there found a man like a merchant (and a merchant he was) who drawing near him, saluted him … Then said the merchant, Sir, I am not acquainted with you, nor you with me, but I have matters of great weight and secresy to impart with you, the which if you will promise … to keep private I will impart with you, if not I will say nothing … Then say on, said Appleyard, I will keep the secret, but what is your name? Nay, said the merchant, by your leave before I tell you my name you shall be sworn upon a book … Now, said the merchant; I am a messenger to you from such persons (and so he named them) in this sort. They say they know you are ungently handled at my Lord of Leicester's hands … If you will join with them who do mind to charge him with certain things, … you shall lack neither gold or silver, and one of the things … is the death of your sister [Amy]; another is that my Lord of Leicester is the only hinderer of the Queen's marriage … And further the merchant said, I will bring you to a house, upon your promise made, where you shall find upon a board 1,000? … and shall have from time to time as much as you shall require … Appleyard answered and said … my Lord of Leicester is better my good lord than he is reported to be. … I will neither for gold or friend stand against him, but am and will be his to death … and so departed.*[7]

So apparently he had been approached by someone who knew secrets concerning Amy's death and who would give him

£1000 to go against Dudley. Blount asked him to name the men involved but he was not forthcoming. Instead William Huggins, who he had been staying with at Hampton Court, had witnessed the meeting and found out that it was 'Norfolk, Sussex, Thomas Heneage and others'.[8]

Blount was sent to bring Appleyard to Dudley where 'the Earl became so angry with Appleyard that it seemed that, if they had been alone, he would have drawn his sword upon him. He bade him depart and to Blount said that he was a very villain'.[9]

But Appleyard had mentioned the Duke of Norfolk and the Earl of Sussex. If there was a plot against Dudley by these men it needed investigating. Appleyard was arrested and sent to the Fleet Prison. He was examined by the Council and it was reported:

> *he said that he had oftentimes moved the Earl to give him leave and to countenance him in the prosecuting of the trial of the murder of his sister, adding that he did take the Earl to be innocent thereof, but yet he thought it an easy matter to find out the offenders, showing certain circumstances which moved him to think surely that she was murdered, whereunto the Earl always answered him that he thought it not fit to deal any further in the matter, considering that by order of law it was already found otherwise, and that it was so presented by a jury.*[10]

Appleyard, in fact, still insisted that 'he had for the Earl's sake covered the murder of his sister'.[11] But something happened to make him change his mind and he realised that he had erred by bringing the names of two peers into the frame.

John Appleyard wrote to the Council on 31 May:

> *This loss of credit with such personages doth drench him in despair. His faults are committed against two noble gentlemen, such as if they had enemies yet their enemies could no ways in honour detect*

them. And he, a caitiff, (in many respects bound to them both) has attempted against duty, love, and troth, yea even against nature, to provoke justly their ires ... Beseeches the Council to be mediators for him to those noble gentlemen against whom he has trespassed and would be much bounden to them if they would give him leave to write either of them one private letter.[12]

But he had not yet given up on having his sister's death investigated and he asked the Council to send him a copy of the coroner's verdict and 'thereupon take counsel's advice how to begin the trial of the cause'.[13]

William Cecil wrote to him on behalf of the Council. They wanted answers and they wanted them in writing.

First how and wherefore you devised the tales that were reported from you to my Lord of Leicester, or certain persons that should solicit you in the name of my Lord of Norfolk's grace, the earl of Sussex and others, to stir up matter against my Lord of Leicester for the death of his wife ... Secondly to declare plainly what moved you to use any speeches to cause the death of the earl of Leicester's wife to be taken as procured by any person; and what you think thereof by the sight of the presentment made by the jury charged by the coroner and now returned into the King's bench. To these matters the Lords would have you answer as plainly in writing at length as you have already done by speech.[14]

On 4 June Appleyard replied but instead of answering all their queries, he wanted the matter dropped. He confirmed to the Council that he had received a copy of the coroner's report into Amy's death and felt:

in which verdict I do find, not only such proofs testified under the oaths of fifteen persons, how my late sister by misfortune happened of death, but also such manifest and plain demonstration thereof,

> *as hath fully and clearly satisfied him and persuaded me; and therefore, my lords, commending her soul to God, I have not further to say of that cause.*

He also acknowledged 'to have received from the Council everything that might bring trial of her unhappy case to light'.[15] He wanted to be released from prison, was sick and had no money.

Appleyard may have had his suspicions but it seems that he changed his mind about his original story or the need to press for anything to be done about Amy's death. Was he truly happy at the outcome or did the conditions he found himself in force him to retract his concerns? More sinisterly did someone convince him to let the matter drop?

At his Star Chamber hearing 'he did confess he accused my Lord of Leicester only of malice ... he fell in rage against my lord & would have accused him ... of killing his wife'.[16] But actually he had never said that Dudley had murdered Amy. In fact he had said that he thought the earl to be innocent but that it would be easy to find the offenders. His reference to the Duke of Norfolk and the Earl of Sussex being behind a plot was glossed over. Appleyard was allowed to walk free. He did not bring up his sister's death again but would die in 1574 under house arrest for his part in a rebellion.

Amy's brother had tried to have her case reopened. He had been sure that foul play had ended her life – that is until the Council and the men that were on it made him change his mind.

Chapter Nine

Murder?

There were several people who had motive to have Amy killed. The issue here is what did they ultimately gain by her death?

Robert Dudley

The prime suspect was Amy's husband who wanted to marry the queen.

Some believe Dudley acted too coldly after his wife's death. He didn't go to the funeral nor have a memorial built for his wife. He acted from a sense of self-preservation and the tone of his letters afterwards show he was concerned mainly for himself.

Given that on the day of the fair Amy wanted the house to herself and she was rushing to have a dress made, some think that she was waiting for a visitor. Could she have been waiting for her husband? It is unlikely that she would have covered up his visit. Usually when he visited Dudley sent food and cooks ahead of him. On this occasion if he was going to kill his wife, he would have visited in secret but Amy surely would have let it slip to one of her maids, at least Mrs Picto, the maid who loved her dearly and served her faithfully or one of the other ladies she shared Cumnor Place with

Dudley anyway had an alibi – he was at court in Windsor, witnessed by many at the time that we can discount him as the murderer.

But of course that doesn't rule out that he didn't arrange Amy's death and have it carried out by someone else. But would he have been so insistent then to have her death investigated? Could he have been so sure that the murderer could not be traced back to him?

Dudley's reactions in the aftermath of Amy's death do not appear those of a man who had something to hide. He wanted Amy's relations, especially her brother-in-law, John Appleyard, to be witness to the inquest. He was insistent that the jury get to the bottom of the matter even if they thought it was by an act of villainy. Even when they declared it was by misfortune, Dudley was anxious to have another inquest to make very sure that their findings could not be refuted. The queen convinced him it was not needed and to let the matter rest.

If Dudley had really wanted Amy dead why would he have not done it sooner? Before the rumours of his relationship with Elizabeth got out of control. Before people had witnessed their growing affection. If Amy had died at the start of Elizabeth's reign, it would not have caused the scandal that it did in 1560.

We have the rumours of him poisoning his wife but they were just rumours, rumours that added to him being Elizabeth's chosen and a possible husband for the queen. If Amy had died of natural causes, Dudley would have been free to marry Elizabeth. The way in which she died, surrounded by suspicion, would mean that his reputation was so tarnished that this could never happen.

The historian James Anthony Froude writing in 1863 came to a different conclusion:

In deference to the general outcry, either the inquiry was portracted, or a second jury, as Dudley suggested was chosen. Lord Robert himself was profoundly anxious, although his anxiety may have been as much for his own reputation as for the discovery of the truth. Yet the exertions to unravel the mystery still failed of their effect. No one could be found who had seen Lady Dudley fall, and she was dead when she was discovered. Eventually, after an investigation apparently without precedent for the strictness with which it had been conducted, the jury returned a verdict of accidental death; and

Lord Robert was thus formally acquitted. Yet the conclusion was evidently of a kind which would not silence suspicion; it was not proved that Lady Dudley had been murdered; but the cause of the death was still left to conjecture ... The conclusion seems inevitable, that, although Dudley was innocent of a direct participation in the crime, the unhappy lady was sacrificed to his ambition. She was murdered by persons who hoped to profit by his elevation to the throne[1]

He agrees there was mystery surrounding Amy's demise but feels that she could have been murdered to ensure Dudley did marry the queen. Perhaps if her death had truly seemed like an accident, it would have been possible but there were too many questions and too much suspicion. He does however also agree that Dudley was innocent of personally committing the crime.

The *Journal of Matters of State* or *BL Additional MS 48023*, an incomplete history, was found in 1978 and instead it pointed to **Sir Richard Verney** as organising the murder by Dudley's 'commandment'.

the Lord Robert's wife brake her neck at Forster's house in Oxfordshire ... her gentlewomen being gone forth to a fair. Howbeit it was thought she was slain, for Sir ----- Varney was there that day and whylest the deed was doing was going over the fair and tarried there for his man, who at length came, and he said, thou knave, why tarriest thou? He answered, should I come before I had done? Hast thou done? quoth Varney. Yeah, quoth the man, I have made it sure...

This Varney and divers others his servants used before her death, to wish her death, which made the people to suspect the worse.[2]

So we have a conversation between Verney and another man at the fair but the author of the *Journal*, possibly John Hales, was not there in person and could not have heard these words spoken. Neither did the author know Robert Dudley as he admits in the text.

Leicester's Commonwealth printed much later in 1584 also pointed to Sir Richard Verney. It could not have got the information from the *Journal* as this collection of material was not printed nor in public circulation. It states that Verney:

> *who by commandment remained with her that day alone, with one man only, and had sent away perforce all her servants from her to a market two miles off, he (I say) with his man can tell how she died, which man, being taken afterward for a felony in the marches of Wales and offering to publish the manner of the said murder, was made away privily in the prison. And Sir Richard himself, dying about the same time in London, cried piteously and blasphemed God, and said to a gentleman of worship of mine acquaintance not long before his death that all the devils in hell did tear him in pieces.*[3]

Verney was based in Warwickshire. Writing to Dudley five months prior to Amy's death he said:

> *I am very sorry that I cannot, according to your Lordship's expectation and my duty, make my repair presently towards you for two principal causes. The one health, which I possess not as I could wish. The other wealth, which doth not abound in me as perhaps is thought.*[4]

So we have a poor, sick man unable to travel. Did he make a recovery and was he then paid off to do away with Amy? There are no other reports that he had any connection to her death but obviously someone had their suspicions. However he was not tainted by rumour at the time as he had sufficient standing to become sheriff in Warwickshire in 1562.

The *Journal of Matters of State* also says:

> *This woman was viewed by the coroner's queste, wherof one Smyth*

was foreman who was the queen's man … and was put out of the house for his lewd behaviour. It was found by this inquest that she was the cause of her own death, falling down a pair of stairs, which by report was but eight steps. But the people say she was killed by reason he forsoke her company without cause and left her first at Hyde's house in Hertfordshire where she said she was poisoned, and for that cause, he desired, she might no longer tarry in his house. From thence she was removed to Varney's house in Warwickshire, and so at length to Foster's house. Many times before it was bruited by the L. Rob... his men that she was dead. And P. (the queen?) used to say that when the Lord Rob. went to his wife he went all in black, and how he was commanded to say that he did nothing with her, when he came to her, as seldom he did.[5]

This is interesting as it points to the foreman of the jury, Sir Richard Smyth, being the queen's man and in fact Dudley had mentioned him to Thomas Blount in a letter written not long after Amy's death:

I have received a letter from one Smythe, one that seemeth to be the foreman of the jury. I perceive by his letters that he and the rest have and do travail very diligently and circumspectly for the trial of that matter which they have charge of, and for any thing that he or they by any search or examination can make in the world hitherto it doth plainly appear, he saith, a very misfortune; which for mine own part … doth much satisfy and quiet me.[6]

Had the queen therefore used her influence to ensure that the jury's findings would be favourable?

Who Else?
Elizabeth I

The queen wanted to marry her favourite.

Elizabeth loved Dudley and she was a jealous queen commanding her favourite to 'not do anything'[7] with his wife. In fact Elizabeth had a long history of being unhappy with those around her having personal relationships. Many of those who married without her permission ended up in the Tower.

When Amy died it was at the height of the queen's infatuation with Dudley. The year 1560 was full of rumours amongst the common people of how close they had become. One John White admitted 'Drunken Burley had said to him in his own house that the Lord Robert Dudley did swive the Queen'.[8] Mother Dowe was arrested for alleging the queen was pregnant with Dudley's child and the vicar of Little Burstead in Essex was in trouble for repeating the rumour that a man had been taken to the Tower for saying the queen was with child.

The queen could do nothing about a wife her favourite had married in his teens. Except Elizabeth could easily arrange to have her killed. Perhaps if Amy had cleared the house of servants she was expecting a secret visit from the queen? If she had been commanded to silence, she would have obeyed. Of course Elizabeth would not be visiting but sending an assassin instead.

Again what would she benefit from Amy's death? A scandalous death? Nothing as she could not afford to be caught in such a scandal. If Elizabeth had been looking for a way to marry Dudley and rid him of his wife surely she would have used an easier method like poison as it had been rumoured. Perhaps Amy's fall was supposed to look like an accident but she had struggled and been hit on the head.

Whereas Dudley's reaction seems to have been shock at his wife's death, the queen's reaction was more suspicious. She had in fact told the Spanish ambassador that 'the Lord Robert's wife was dead, or nearly so'[9] before it became public knowledge. We can assume though that she had actually heard the news. Dudley would have told her immediately of the messenger from Cumnor but before he knew any more from Blount's reports. The Duke of Norfolk had also told the ambassador that Elizabeth had told him she would be married before six months were out but she didn't say to whom.

Her conversation with Robert Jones is even more sinister. Whilst explaining that in the matter of Amy's death there was nothing to touch Dudley's honour she mentioned the 'attempt' on Amy's life. Why would she say that if she didn't have suspicions herself or knew more than she let on?

In November 1560 the rumours were definitely taking their toll. The queen was reported as 'not looking so hearty and well as she did, by a great deal, and surely the matter of my lord Robert doth much perplex her'.[10]

Elizabeth is supposed to have told Dudley when she was young that she would never marry but at the height of her infatuation with her Master of Horse she may well have toyed with the idea of Dudley as her husband. She enjoyed his attention and encouraged him to believe they had a future together. She certainly put Kat Ashley down for trying to make her give up her favourite.

Would she really have risked everything for Dudley? Surely her brush with Seymour had taught her a lesson she would never forget. Although Elizabeth was adamant with Kat, her closest companion, that she deserved Dudley's affection, she began to realise how much their relationship was talked about by ambassadors and across the courts of Europe. If she had had any involvement in Amy's death, she ultimately gained nothing from it.

* * *

So was Amy waiting for a secret visitor that turned out to be her murderer? Was it a lover's tryst gone wrong? Amy was deeply religious and her life was one that was monitored by the several people she shared a household with. It is highly unlikely that she had a lover. She could have been waiting for someone else, someone who had a message for her and there were several men who could have set this up, who hated Dudley and saw Amy's death as a route to his downfall.

Dudley had his enemies. Many were not happy at the rise of a man who was derogatively known as 'the gypsy' and came from a family tainted by treason. As we have seen by the ambassador's reports, they thought Dudley was eager to see his wife die so that he could marry the queen and that is exactly what the next three suspects have in common.

There were men who would do anything to stop Dudley becoming king.

Thomas Howard, 4th Duke of Norfolk hated Dudley – Quadra wrote that he was 'the chief of Lord Robert's enemies, who are all the principal people in the kingdom and that he had said that if Lord Robert did not abandon his present pretentions and presumptions, he would not die in his bed … I think his hatred of Lord Robert will continue, as the Duke and the rest of them cannot put up with his being king'.[11]

Howard was the son of the poet Henry Howard, the Earl of Surrey, who was beheaded on 19 January 1547 on a charge of treason for quartering the royal arms. His grandfather was the infamous 3rd Duke of Norfolk who had also been in the Tower but was released after Henry VIII's death. Through his family connections Howard was second cousin to the queen and after his grandfather's death he became the 4th Duke of Norfolk.

His relationship with the queen's favourite had started well enough. Norfolk and Dudley both served the queen at her coronation on 15 January 1599; Norfolk as Earl Marshal and Dudley as Master of Horse. In these roles they would often be called on to attend state occasions. Together they were made knights of the garter in the following April but already there were rumours that Norfolk was jealous of Dudley and the attention and favours the queen bestowed on him. Norfolk found some respite from court when he returned to his home at Kenninghall to deal with his vast estate.

When Norfolk returned to court in the autumn of 1559 he was appalled to see just how intimate Dudley had become with the queen. Along with his friends Sussex and Cecil he shared a dread of what might happen if she should ever marry her Master of Horse.

Dudley was gaining more and more power and interfering in matters Norfolk felt he shouldn't. The duke's complaints against him were growing. Through Dudley's influence, John Appleyard, Amy's half-brother had been appointed to the position of High Sheriff of Norfolk in place of the man the duke had deemed suitable for the role.

When it came to paying the Parliamentary subsidy, Norfolk had been assessed as one of the top three highest paying peers in the kingdom but Dudley wasn't assessed at all. He had a writ of discharge from the queen. Something that rankled Norfolk so much he refused to pay his dues for a time. Norfolk could not contain his disdain for the queen's favourite and people were beginning to notice their enmity.

It was reported in October 1559 that:

A plot was made the other day to murder Lord Robert and it is now common talk and threat. The plot was headed by the Duke of Norfolk, the Earl of Sussex and all the principal adherents of the scheme for marrying the Queen to the Archduke. The Queen and Lord Robert are very uneasy about the Duke of Norfolk as he talks openly about her lightness and bad government. People are ashamed of what is going on, and particularly the duke, as he is Lord Robert's enemy.[12]

There is no evidence that Norfolk was involved or if this plot really existed. Norfolk wanted Dudley's downfall so would he have considered killing the queen's favourite? It would be difficult to kill a man who was so often in the queen's presence and never far from her royal highness. His wife, however, would be easier to target. Perhaps there had been another plot. One to discredit Dudley and make sure that he never married the queen. There is no proof, no evidence but Norfolk was Dudley's chief enemy and he had the motive and the means to murder his wife.

Norfolk was commander of the English army in Scotland up until July 1560. During this time he built up his relationship with Cecil who was working towards a peace treaty and spending time on diplomatic duties north of the border. Both men were rumoured to have been given this thankless task due to Dudley's influence and neither were happy about it.

There is no known response from Norfolk on Amy's death, after which the duke and Dudley continued to loathe each other. Even their servants quarrelled. Dudley once wrote to Norfolk that his servants were declaring him their master's enemy and if this were not true, he wanted them reprimanded. But of course it was true.

There was no let-up in the animosity that Norfolk and Dudley shared. In 1565 they managed to play a game of tennis in the queen's presence when

> *my Lord Robert being hot and sweating took the Queen's napkin out of her hand and wiped his face, which the Duke seeing said that he was too saucy, and swore that he would lay his racket upon his face; whereup rose a great trouble and the Queen offended sore with the Duke…*[13]

Amy was long gone and if Norfolk had any hand in her death, it hadn't stopped the problem of Dudley from still festering. Dudley had promised to back down as negotiations for the queen's marriage to the archduke Charles went ahead. Before

Norfolk left court in December 1565 he told Elizabeth any advice she had had to marry Dudley was 'not because they really thought the match would be beneficial to the country, or good for her own dignity'.[14] Elizabeth let it pass but as soon as Norfolk returned to court in January 1566, Norfolk and Dudley were at war again.

When parliament met in September 1566 the thorny issue of the succession was broached and in a joint effort of the Lords and the Commons Elizabeth was pressed to make a decision. Norfolk was their spokesman.

> *The Queen was so angry that she addressed hard words to the Duke of Norfolk, whom she called traitor or conspirator, or other words of similar flavour. He replied that he never thought to have to ask her pardon for having offended her thus ... Pembroke remarked to her that it was not right to treat the Duke badly, since he and others were only doing what was fitting for the good of the country, and advising her what was best for her, and if she did not think fit to adopt the advice, it was still their duty to offer it. She told him he talked like a swaggering soldier, and said to Leicester that she had thought if all the world abandoned her he would not have done so, to which he answered that he would die at her feet; and she said that had nothing to do with the matter.*[15]

Elizabeth was thoroughly peeved with them all but days later she agreed to discuss the matter and assured them that she would marry, hinting it would probably be to the Archduke Charles, as soon as she could.

It is interesting to note that by now the rumours of her marrying Dudley had died down and when it came to matters of state, she would not brook even his interference.

Norfolk was on his own path to destruction. As far back as 1564, the queen had suggested he could be a possible husband for Mary Queen of Scots, as she had also done with Dudley.

Whereas Mary believed Dudley to be a nobody, Norfolk held more interest as being England's premier peer.

In 1568 the Scottish ambassador Maitland approached him to resurrect the possibility of his marriage. Unfortunately Norfolk failed to inform Elizabeth I and was arrested and sent to the Tower in 1569. After his release the following year he became embroiled in the Ridolfi plot which would lead to his downfall.

Ridolfi was an Italian banker and an ardent Catholic. He ran messages between King Philip II, Pope Pius V, Mary Queen of Scots and Norfolk. His aim was to engineer the overthrow of Elizabeth and to restore the true religion and set Mary Queen of Scots on the throne.

The plan was 10,000 Spanish troops would invade England under the command of the Duke of Alba who were garrisoned in the Netherlands. Joining with the Catholic nobility they would work to put Mary on the throne and Howard would rule by her side.

Norfolk had turned from his queen in exasperation. He had been a loyal and solid supporter and it seems incredible that he would become involved in a plot to see Elizabeth murdered. Whatever the truth of the matter, his dealings with Mary Queen of Scots led to his arrest and execution in 1572. As he stood before the block he gave a lengthy speech denying his guilt and swearing he was never a papist. Elizabeth had delayed his execution for as long as she could. He was her cousin and the highest peer in the realm but treason could not go unpunished and Howard would die with one swing of the axe, taking his secrets with him.

Another man who loathed Dudley and feared him marrying the queen was **Thomas Radcliffe, the 3rd Earl of Sussex**. Born around 1526, Sussex had served Mary I as Lord Deputy of Ireland. He continued to serve Elizabeth as Lord Lieutenant of Ireland in 1560 but was often at court. He was a military careerist and his enmity towards Dudley 'his professed antagonist to his dying day'[16] was well known. Sussex was of noble birth and related to the queen through his aunt Elizabeth Howard, mother of Anne Boleyn and he felt Dudley was beneath him. 'In the bosom of the high-born Sussex there mingled an illiberal disdain of the origin of Dudley, with a just abhorrence of his whole character and conduct'.[17]

Sussex shared his animosity with Norfolk. Cecil once wrote 'my Lord of Norfolk loveth my Lord of Sussex earnestly, and so all that stock of the Howards seem to join in friendship together'.[18] It's not hard to imagine they also joined in plotting against Dudley and working to ensure their queen married someone more suitable.

More than anything Sussex was loyal to his queen. Could he have arranged Amy's death to save her from making a terrible mistake? He was appalled that the queen could even contemplate marrying Dudley and much favoured Charles II, archduke of Austria, as Norfolk had done, as a more appropriate suitor.

In 1561 the Earl of Sussex became resigned to the possibility that the queen might marry her favourite and wrote to Cecil giving this advice:

I wish not her Majesty to linger this matter of so great importance, but to choose speedily; and therein to follow so much her own affection as (that), by the looking upon him whom she should choose, omnes ejus sensus titillarentur (all the senses being excited); which shall be the readiest way, with the help of God, to bring us a blessed prince which shall redeem us out of thraldom. If I knew that England had other rightful inheritors I would then advise otherwise, and seek to serve the time by a husband's choice. But seeing that she is ultimum refugium, and that no riches, friendship, foreign alliance, or any other present commodity that might come by a husband, can serve our turn, without issue of her body, if the Queen will love anybody, let her love where and whom she lists, so much thirst I to see her love. And whomsoever she shall love and choose, him will I love, honour, and serve to the uttermost.[19]

What he wrote was a complete turnaround. Was he only saying that knowing it was not a possibility now? Did his seeming acquiescence cover up a dastardly deed?

Later the Spanish ambassador Diego Guzmán de Silva would say of Sussex and Cecil that they were 'no friends to Lord Robert in their hearts'.[20] Cecil would often note in his diary when Sussex and Dudley quarrelled and in 1566 at Greenwich their tempers boiled over in front of the queen. Sussex would continue to have furious quarrels with Elizabeth's favourite especially after he was made Lord Chamberlain in 1572 and spent more time at court. The queen would often try to mediate between the two.

When Dudley's marriage to Lettice Knollys came to the queen's knowledge, Sussex is supposed to have prevented him from being sent to the Tower. But this story often quoted was not printed until 1615 in William Camden's *Annales* and seems to be the only source for Sussex acting on Dudley's behalf. This seems hardly likely given their relationship although he could afford to be magnanimous. With Dudley married again it put to an end any more speculation he would marry the queen.

On his death bed in 1583 Sussex is reported to have said 'beware of the gypsy for he will be too hard for you all; you know not the beast so well as I do'.[21]

William Cecil, the Queen's chief advisor and Secretary of State, who had also served the Lord Protector, Edward Seymour and Edward VI, had reason to blacken Dudley's name. He struggled to advise a queen who put her favourite first, who worked her secretary into exhaustion and steadfastly refused to marry possible suitors.

He had been with Elizabeth from the beginning. He had never taken a role in Mary I's reign and had remained Elizabeth's staunch supporter and financial advisor. It was well known that on her succession he would take a primary role. The Spanish ambassador at the time, de Feria, wrote 'I have been told for certain that Cecil, who was King Edward's secretary, will also be secretary to madame Elizabeth. He is said to be an able and virtuous man, but a heretic...'[22] At her first council meeting of her reign she created him Secretary of State.

Cecil hoped that 'God would send our mistress a husband, and by and by a son, that we may hope our posterity shall have a masculine succession'[23] but he also hoped that that would not be Dudley.

After Cecil returned from his diplomatic embassy to Scotland where he stayed for over two months to finalise the Treaty of Edinburgh, he was appalled to see how close the queen had become to her favourite. He told the Spanish ambassador:

> *After exacting many pledges of strict secrecy, he said that the Queen was conducting herself in such a way that he thought of retiring. He said it was a bad sailor who did not enter port if he could when he saw a storm coming on, and he clearly foresaw the ruin of the realm through Robert's intimacy with the Queen, who surrendered all affairs to him and meant to marry him. He said he did not know how the country put up with it, and he should ask leave to go home, though he thought they would cast him into the Tower first. He ended by begging me in God's name to point out to the Queen the effect of her misconduct, and persuade her not to abandon business entirely, but to look to her realm; and then he repeated to me twice over that Lord Robert would be better in Paradise than here.*[24]

The situation had gotten so bad that Cecil was considering giving up. He told the Earl of Bedford, 'The court is as I left it, and therefore do I mind to leave it as I have too much cause, if I durst write all. As soon as I can get Sir Nicholas Throgmorton placed, so soon I purpose to withdraw myself...'[25]

Even Quadra thought the situation so disastrous someone

would 'do something to set this crooked business straight'.[26] So perhaps Cecil also considered what he could do about the situation and in his frustration and fear he arranged Amy's demise.

His conversations with the Spanish ambassador were that of a frustrated man true but also a clever and astute man. Cecil told Quadra what he knew would be repeated. When he told him Amy was in good health and protecting herself from poison, was he setting up the situation so that her demise would be a shock? And when he told him Amy was dead prior to a public announcement was he adding a hint of suspicion? His talks with the ambassador smack of pre-planning and manipulation.

Cecil wasn't just afraid for his queen and her virtue, he was afraid for his country. He feared that if Elizabeth was overthrown, Mary Queen of Scots would be placed on the throne, making England once again a Catholic country. Was he even hedging his bets with Quadra building on a relationship with Spain in case this came to be? (Much later he would cover up his dealings with Spain in the case of Dr Lopez).

In 1567 the Earl of Oxford killed an under-cook Thomas Brincknell in the gardens of Cecil House. Oxford was practising his fencing skills when, as the jury found, Brincknell fell on his rapier killing himself instantly. Of course it was improbable that the cook had just run into Oxford's blade causing such a severe injury but the jury were convinced to rule he had committed suicide. Oxford would go on to marry Cecil's daughter and the queen's secretary would later admit 'I did my best to have the jury find the death of a poor man whom he killed in my house to be found se defendendo'[27] – that Oxford had acted in self-defence. This incident shows Cecil was not above influencing the findings of a jury and manipulating its outcome.

Cecil would go on to urge Elizabeth to execute Mary Queen of Scots. When she delayed he convened a secret meeting of the Privy Council to ensure Mary's death warrant was sent to

Fotheringhay. He may even have been involved in organising the murder of Mary's second husband, Darnley.

Recent investigation has also linked him with the death of the playwright Christopher Marlowe in 1593. Marlowe was stabbed in what appeared to be a drink-fuelled brawl but the men involved; Ingram Frizer, Nicholas Keres and Robert Poley as well as Marlowe were all caught up in the Elizabethan spy network. It has been suggested that Marlowe knew too much, especially about Cecil and his son Robert, enough to bring them down and have them tried for heresy.

Cecil dealt with threats to realm in the best way he saw fit – by eliminating them. Cecil did not want Dudley marrying the queen and saw their relationship as a threat. Where the death of Amy might have left Dudley free to remarry, the way in which it was committed and the suspicion surrounding it meant Dudley was now stained by the rumours abounding of how she died and who might have killed her. Cecil later put his thoughts down on paper entitled 'Reasons against the Earl of Leicester' and he listed:

> *Nothing is increased by marriage to him either in riches, estimation, power.*
>
> *It will be thought that the slanderous speeches of the Queen with the Earl have been true.*
>
> *He shall study nothing but to enhance his own particular friends: to wealth, to offices, to lands and to offend others.*
>
> *He is infamed by the death of his wife.*
>
> *He is far in debt.*
>
> *He is like to prove unkind or jealous of the Queen's majesty*[28]

After Amy's death, Cecil went from being out of favour with the queen to being the one man she could trust and confide in. Dudley needed him desperately too. There was no more talk of resigning.

* * *

Cecil, Norfolk and Sussex could have been complicit in making sure that Dudley was so tainted with scandal, he could never marry the queen. It would be a plot at the highest level but one that each of these men could easily have seen played out.

Whether these men had anything to do with Amy's death is a matter of conjecture but they all three had reason to see Dudley taken down.

Any one of them, or together, had the strongest motive to arrange Amy's death.

Chapter Ten

Ongoing Rumours

After Appleyard raised the issue of Amy's death, no more was said of the matter – at least publicly – until 1584 when what is now known as *Leicester's Commonwealth* was published. Sir Francis Walsingham was the first to tell Dudley of 'a printed libel against your Lordship, the most malicious-written thing that ever was penned since the beginning of the world'.[1] It was first printed in Paris or Antwerp probably the work of Charles Arundell and a group of Catholic dissidents.

The savage attack on Dudley's character was written in the form of a conversation between three men and as well as detailing his numerous faults it also blamed him for Amy's murder saying 'His Lordship changeth wives and minions, by killing the one…'[2]

Dudley was, at that time it suggests, 'yet not so stony harted as to appoint out the particular manner of her death, but rather to leave that, to the discretion of the murderer'. This as we have seen was supposedly Sir Richard Verney who 'should first attempt to kill her by poison, and if that tooke not place then by any other way to dispatch her, howsoever'. The writer of *Leicester's Commonwealth* gave proof of this as coming from one Dr Walter Bayly who it had been hoped would administer poison 'the Italian art'. The conspirators who wanted Amy dead – Dudley's men – had tried to persuade her to take a potion but when that failed they called in Dr Bayly to try and give her something 'meaning to have added also somewhat of their owne'. The doctor suspected something was amiss and 'flatly denied their request, misdoubting (as he after reported) least if they had poisoned her under the name of his potion: he might after have been hanged for a cover of their sin'.[3]

Bayly was well known at court. He had given a talk on poison that the queen attended as the pamphlet described:

> *For I heard him once myself in a public act in Oxford (and that in the presence of Leicester, if I not be deceived) maintain that poison might be so tempered and given as it should not appear presently, and yet should kill the party afterward at which time I should be appointed.*[4]

He had been Dudley's doctor in the 1570s and the earl had recommended him to the queen when she was suffering from one of her dreadful toothaches. He had later joined her group of physicians and was trusted with her care.

Bayly did not confirm or deny his involvement with Amy as far as we know. As Elizabeth had *Leicester's Commonwealth* suppressed he may have been ordered to keep quiet and not rise to comment. It may be that there was at least some truth in the allegations and he had at least visited Amy as her doctor.

The queen did respond to the publication however, denouncing it not once but twice and giving a statement:

> *The very same and divers other such like most slanderous, shameful, and devilish books and libels have been continually spread abroad and kept by disobedient persons, to the manifest contempt of her majesty's regal and sovereign authority, and namely, among the rest, one most infamous containing slanderous and hateful matter against our very good Lord the earl of Leicester, one of her principal noblemen and Chief Counsellor of State, of which most malicious and wicked imputations, her Majesty in her own clear knowledge doth declare and testify his innocence to all the world.*[5]

Other pamphlets followed in its wake. A 'Letter of Estate' published in 1585 had this to say

The good lady being at her [house in] the country, full slenderly accompanied, as one [meant] towards small good, her lord seldom or never vis[iting] her, this lamentable inc[ident o]ne day fell out. As two of her gentle se[rvants were in the] parlor playing at tables for there [recreation, as] also to pass [the] time away withal, [they pause in] their [talk] and to their plain hearing someth[ing falls] down the stairs, whereat the [one] jesting says to the other down for a shilling, the other lik[ewi]se merely answering up for another. And so [they continue]d in playing their game until the same [was] finish[ed] and ended, little suspecting what was fal[len.] And now their game being come [to an] end, and hearing no body make any [move to] take up what was fallen, one of them steppe[d to the] stair's foot to see what it should be. W[hat to their] appalled sperites there appeared unto them, the corpse of that noble lady without breath, se[eming to have] her neck bone broke in sunder, th[e murderers escaped] and gone past hue and [cry, who for] the reward of their [evil labours may] the Lorde throw do[wn vengeance from] above upon so foul and wicked murders, as also on him which set them a work, to his perpetual reproach and infamy. But now to colour [the] matter withal, most falsely and slanderously it [is] given forth that she fell by chance down the stairs and brake h[er neck, which is] a likely matter, a lady to fall down [the stair]s and never heard cry, her neck to [be broken but with no] blood spilt. But his Lordship said [so, and then] who durste say the contr[ary.] Much mutte[ring] there was about this sudden death of hers, but [no] man durste say a word for his life.[6]

Interestingly this is the only account to mention there was no blood spilt.

The following year a pamphlet entitled 'Flores Calvinistici' talked again about Amy's murder but this time with the added flourish that she was 'destroyed by a small nail thrust gradually into her head'.[7]

Further accounts appeared over the years but they were

becoming removed from the events until there was no one left who could have known the truth.

Dudley had married the widowed Lettice Knollys, daughter of Sir Francis Knollys and Catherine Carey in September 1578. When the queen had found out she had been furious banning Lettice from ever coming into her presence and almost sending Dudley to the Tower. But their relationship had rallied and as they grew older, they remained close. On his death in 1588 Elizabeth was devastated. He was the one man that she had truly loved. Elizabeth I of course would live out a long and glorious reign until her death in 1603 at Richmond Palace. She never did marry and although she had other favourites no one ever came as close to her as Dudley had done.

Stories of Amy's demise continued. Antony Wood writing in 1658 did at least visit Cumnor and came away with the tale that Amy had been given a different bed chamber for the night. The bed was positioned so its head was by a privy postern door and her murderers snuck in stifled her, bruised her head, broke her neck and then flung her down the stairs.

Elias Ashmole writing in 1719 repeated the story of a door by the bed but this time a spit was used to damage her head before she was thrown down the stairs. He felt that Dudley and Anthony Forster had plotted her death.

The mystery of Amy's death would be fictionalised in *Kenilworth* by Sir Walter Scott and more recently in Philippa Gregory's *The Virgin Lover* and *The Marriage Game* by Alison Weir.

Amy's memory would live on – an Elizabethan mystery that would continue to fascinate authors and readers alike.

The death of Amy Robsart is one of those mysteries that will probably never be solved. We can't gauge how she was feeling nor know if her body was failing her. Several people had reason to discredit her husband and may have seen her death as a way to do so but Dudley himself does not seem a likely culprit. There are amongst others – William Cecil, Thomas Howard, the 4th

Duke of Norfolk and Thomas Radcliffe, the 3rd Earl of Sussex – who did have reason to see Amy dead and Dudley discredited.

Accident, suicide, or murder – what do you think?

Thus sore and sad that ladie griev'd,
In Cumnor Halle so lone and dreare;
And manye a heartefelte sighe shee heav'd
And let falle manye a bitter teare.

And ere the dawne of daye appear'd,
In Cumnor Hall so lone and dreare,
Full manye a piercing screame was hearde,
And manye a crye of mortal feare.

The death-belle thrice was hearde to ring,
An aërial voyce was hearde to call,
And thrice the raven flapp'd its wyng
Arounde the tow'rs of Cumnor Hall.

The mastiffe howl'd at village doore,
The oaks were shatter'd on the greene;
Woe was the houre--for never more
That haplesse countesse e'er was seene.

And in that manor now no more
Is chearful feaste and sprightly balle;
For ever since that dhearye houre
Have spirits haunted Cumnor Hall.

From 'Cumnor Hall', a poem by William Mickle.

References

Chapter One: The Wife of Elizabeth I's Favourite

1. Adams, Leicester and the Court
2. CSP Spain
3. Ibid.
4. Weir, *Elizabeth the Queen*
5. CSP Spain
6. Weir, *Elizabeth the Queen*
7. Skidmore, *Death and the Virgin*
8. CSP Spain
9. Weir, *Elizabeth the Queen*
10. Skidmore, *Death and the Virgin*
11. Ibid.

Chapter Two: The Ambassador's Reports

1. CSP Spain
2. CSP Venice
3. CSP Spain
4. Skidmore, *Death and the Virgin*
5. Ibid.
6. CSP Spain
7. Ibid.

Chapter Three: The Aftermath

1. Adlard, Amye Robsart
2. Ibid.
3. Skidmore, *Death and the Virgin*
4. Ibid.
5. Ibid.
6. Ibid.
7. Ibid.
8. Ibid.

9. Adams, Leicester and the Court
10. Ibid.
11. CSP Spain
12. Ibid.
13. *Leicester's Commonwealth*
14. Skidmore, *Death and the Virgin*
15. Wood, *The History and Antiquities of the University of Oxford*

Chapter Four: Rumours Surround the Queen

1. Whitelock, *Elizabeth's Bedfellows*
2. *Calendar of State Papers, Foreign*
3. Ibid.
4. Skidmore, *Death and the Virgin*
5. Ibid.
6. Ibid.
7. Froude, *History of England from the Fall of Wolsey to the Death of Elizabeth*

Chapter Five: The Coroner's Report

1. https://www.nationalarchives.gov.uk/education/resources/elizabeth-monarchy/coroners-report/

Chapter Six: Accident?

1. Skidmore, *Death and the Virgin*
2. *Leicester's Commonwealth*
3. Office of National Statistics
4. Skidmore, *Death and the Virgin*
5. Wilson, *Sweet Robin*

Chapter Seven: Suicide?

1. Wilson, *The Uncrowned Kings of England*
2. Skidmore, *Death and the Virgin*
3. Ibid.
4. Bernard, *Power and Politics in Tudor England*

5. Archer (ed.), Religion, Politics, and Society in Sixteenth-Century England.
6. Skidmore, *Death and the Virgin*
7. Picard, *Elizabeth's London*

Chapter Eight: The Curious Case of John Appleyard

1. CSP Spain
2. CSP Venice
3. Skidmore, *Death and the Virgin*
4. Ibid.
5. CSP Spain
6. *English Historical Review*
7. Ibid.
8. Ibid.
9. HMC, Pepys MSS
10. Cecil Papers
11. Weir, *Elizabeth the Queen*
12. Cecil Papers
13. Ibid.
14. Skidmore, *Death and the Virgin*
15. Bernard, *Power and Politics in Tudor England*
16. Skidmore, *Death and the Virgin*

Chapter Nine: Murder?

1. Froude, *History of England from the Fall of Wolsey to the Death of Elizabeth*
2. *Journal of Matters of State*
3. *Leicester's Commonwealth*
4. Skidmore, *Death and the Virgin*
5. *Journal of Matters of State*
6. Adlard, Amye Robsart
7. *Leicester's Commonwealth*
8. Whitelock, *Elizabeth's Bedfellows*
9. CSP Spain

10. Doran, *Elizabeth I and Her Circle*
11. CSP Spain
12. Skidmore, *Death and the Virgin*
13. Froude, *History of England from the Fall of Wolsey to the Death of Elizabeth*
14. Weir, *Elizabeth the Queen*
15. CSP Spain
16. Naunton, *Fragmenta regalia*
17. Aikin, *Memoirs of the Court of Queen Elizabeth*
18. Wilson, *Sweet Robin*
19. Whitelock, *Elizabeth's Bedfellows*
20. CSP Spain
21. Naunton, Sir Richard, *Fragmenta regalia*
22. CSP Spain
23. Weir, *Elizabeth the Queen*
24. CSP Spain
25. Wilson, *Sweet Robin*
26. CSP Spain
27. Rowse, *Eminent Elizabethans*
28. Loades, *The Cecils*

Chapter Ten: Ongoing Rumours

1. Skidmore, *Death and the Virgin*
2. *Leicester's Commonwealth*
3. Ibid.
4. Ibid.
5. Adlard, Amye Robsart
6. https://www.dpeck.info/write/leter.htm
7. Skidmore, *Death and the Virgin*

Select Bibliography

Adams, Simon, Leicester and the Court: Essays in Elizabethan Politics. Manchester, 2002

Adlard, George, Amye Robsart and the Earl of Leycester, London, 1870

Aikin, Lucy, *Memoirs of the Court of Queen Elizabeth*, Luton, 2010

Archer, I. W. (ed), *Religion, Politics and Society in Sixteenth-Century England*, Cambridge, 2003

Bernard, G. W., *Power and Politics in Tudor England*, London, 2000

Borman, Tracy: *Elizabeth's Women*, London, 2009

British History Online, www.british-history.ac.uk

Calendar of State Papers, Domestic (Edward, Mary and Elizabeth)

Calendar of State Papers, Foreign

Calendar of State Papers, Venice

Cecil Papers

Devereux/ Dudley Papers

Doran, Susan, *Elizabeth I and Her Circle*, Oxford, 2015

Dunn, Jane: *Elizabeth & Mary*, London, 2003

Erickson, Carolly: *The First Elizabeth*, London, 1999

Froude, James Anthony, *History of England from the Fall of Wolsey to the Death of Elizabeth*, Cambridge, 1870

Gristwood, Sarah, *Elizabeth & Leicester*, London, 2007

Hartweg, Christine, *Amy Robsart: A Life and Its End*, CreateSpace, 2017

HMC, Pepys MSS

Jenkins, Elizabeth, *Elizabeth & Leicester*, London, 1961

Journal of Matters of State or *BL Additional MS 48023*

Laurence, Anne: *Women in England 1500–1760 A Social History*, London, 1994

Leicester's Commonwealth

Loades, David, *The Cecils*, London, 2007

Mortimer, Ian: *The Time Traveller's Guide to Elizabethan England*,

London, 2012

Naunton, Sir Richard, *Fragmenta regalia, or, Observations on the late Queen Elizabeth, her times and favorits*, London, 1641

Nicholl, Charles, *The Reckoning: The Murder of Christopher Marlowe*, London, 1992

Papers relating to Mary Queen of Scots, ed. William Knollys, Philobiblon Society

Miscellanies, 14-15, 1872–6

Parliament Online, www.historyofparliamentonline.org

Perry, Maria: *The Word of a Prince: A Life of Elizabeth I*, Woodbridge, 1990

Picard, Liza, *Elizabeth's London*, London, 2004

Plowden, Alison: *The Young Elizabeth*, Stroud, 1971

Read, Conyers: *Mr Secretary Cecil and Queen Elizabeth*, London, 1955

Ridley, Jasper: *Elizabeth I*, London, 1987

Rowse, A. L., *Eminent Elizabethans*, New York, 1983

Skidmore, Chris, *Death and the Virgin*, London, 2010

Starkey, David: *Elizabeth*, London, 2000

Somerset, Anne: *Elizabeth I*, London, 1991

Somerset, Anne: *Ladies in Waiting*, London, 1984

'The Death of Amy Robsart' in *The English Historical Review*, Vol. 1, No. 2 (Apr., 1886), pp. 235–259

Weir, Alison: *Elizabeth the Queen*, London, 1998

Whitelock, Anna: *Elizabeth's Bedfellows*, Bloomsbury, 2013

Williams, Neville, *Thomas Howard Fourth Duke of Norfolk*, London, 1964

Wilson, Derek, *Sweet Robin: A Biography of Robert Dudley Earl of Leicester 1533–1588*, London, 1997

Wilson, Derek, *The Uncrowned Kings of England: The Black Legend of the Dudleys*, London, 2005

Wood, Anthony, *The History and Antiquities of the University of Oxford*, Oxford, 1795

CHRONOS
BOOKS

HISTORY

Chronos Books is an historical non-fiction imprint. Chronos publishes real history for real people; bringing to life people, places and events in an imaginative, easy-to-digest and accessible way - histories that pass on their stories to a generation of new readers.

If you have enjoyed this book, why not tell other readers by posting a review on your preferred book site.

Recent bestsellers from Chronos Books are:

Lady Katherine Knollys

The Unacknowledged Daughter of King Henry VIII

Sarah-Beth Watkins

A comprehensive account of Katherine Knollys' questionable paternity, her previously unexplored life in the Tudor court and her intriguing relationship with Elizabeth I.

Paperback: 978-1-78279-585-8 ebook: 978-1-78279-584-1

Cromwell was Framed

Ireland 1649

Tom Reilly

Revealed: The definitive research that proves the Irish nation owes Oliver Cromwell a huge posthumous apology for wrongly convicting him of civilian atrocities in 1649.

Paperback: 978-1-78279-516-2 ebook: 978-1-78279-515-5

Why the CIA Killed JFK and Malcolm X

The Secret Drug Trade in Laos

John Koerner

A new groundbreaking work presenting evidence that the CIA silenced JFK to protect its secret drug trade in Laos.

Paperback: 978-1-78279-701-2 ebook: 978-1-78279-700-5

The Disappearing Ninth Legion

A Popular History

Mark Olly

The Disappearing Ninth Legion examines hard evidence for the foundation, development, mysterious disappearance, or possible continuation of Rome's lost Legion.

Paperback: 978-1-84694-559-5 ebook: 978-1-84694-931-9

Beaten But Not Defeated

Siegfried Moos - A German anti-Nazi who settled in Britain

Merilyn Moos

Siegi Moos, an anti-Nazi and active member of the German Communist Party, escaped Germany in 1933 and, exiled in Britain, sought another route to the transformation of capitalism.

Paperback: 978-1-78279-677-0 ebook: 978-1-78279-676-3

A Schoolboy's Wartime Letters

An evacuee's life in WWII — A Personal Memoir

Geoffrey Iley

A boy writes home during WWII, revealing his own fascinating story, full of zest for life, information and humour.

Paperback: 978-1-78279-504-9 ebook: 978-1-78279-503-2

The Life & Times of the Real Robyn Hoode

Mark Olly

A journey of discovery. The chronicles of the genuine historical character, Robyn Hoode, and how he became one of England's greatest legends.

Paperback: 978-1-78535-059-7 ebook: 978-1-78535-060-3

Readers of ebooks can buy or view any of these bestsellers by clicking on the live link in the title. Most titles are published in paperback and as an ebook. Paperbacks are available in traditional bookshops. Both print and ebook formats are available online.

Find more titles and sign up to our readers' newsletter at http://www.johnhuntpublishing.com/history-home

Follow us on Facebook at https://www.facebook.com/ChronosBooks

and Twitter at https://twitter.com/ChronosBooks